D0603900

## Play Time

# Let's Play Tag

## By Sarah Hughes

Welcome Books

Children's Press
A Division of Grolier Publishing
New York / London / Hong Kong / Sydney
Danbury, Connecticut

Photo Credits: Cover and all photos by Maura Boruchow
Contributing Editor: Mark Beyer
Book Design: Michael DeLisio

Visit Children's Press on the Internet at:
http://publishing.grolier.com

Library of Congress Cataloging-in-Publication Data

Hughes, Sarah, 1964-
   Let's play tag / by Sarah Hughes.
      p. cm. — (Play time)
   Includes bibliographical references and index.
   Summary: A group of children play tag and explain the rules.
   ISBN 0-516-23116-2 (lib. bdg.) — ISBN 0-516-23041-7 (pbk.)
   1. Tag games—Juvenile literature. [1. Tag games. 2. Games.] I. Title.

GV1207.H84 2000
796—dc21

                                                              00-025910

# Contents

My name is Carlos.

I'm with my friends at the **playground**.

Their names are Maria, Dawn, Kim, and Andre.

We have enough people to play **tag**.

I call, "You're **it**!" and tag Andre.

The others run away.

7

We run back and forth.

We try not to get caught.

If you are caught, you will be "it."

If you get tired, go to the **base**.

It is a good spot to rest.

You can catch your breath.

Andre catches up to Kim.

He tags her.

Now she's "it."

Dawn likes to wait on the bridge.

I wonder if Kim will chase after her?

Kim might chase after me.

15

"I'm going to get you!" Kim yells.

She points at Dawn.

17

Kim runs up on the bridge.

Dawn runs to the slide.

I think Kim is going to catch Dawn.

18

19

Kim did it!

She tagged Dawn.

Tag is fun to play at the park.

21

# New Words

**base** (**bays**) a safe place from being tagged

**it** (**it**) the person who must tag one of the others

**playground** (**play**-grownd) a place with slides, swing sets, and other playthings

**tag** (**tag**) a game in which you have to chase and touch a person

# To Find Out More

**Books**
*Rain or Shine Activity Book: Fun Things to Make & Do*
By Joanna Cole, Stephanie Calmenson and Alan Tiegreen
William Morrow & Company

*The Big Book of Games*
by Dorothy M. Stott
Dutton Books

**Web Sites**
**Games Kids Play**
http://www.gameskidsplay.net
This page has a list of many games that kids can play. The rules are given for each game.

**Richardson School – Best Games in a Small World**
http://www.richardsonps.act.edu.au
Learn new games to play at this site. It includes the rules for each game.

**23**

# Index

**About the Author**
Sarah Hughes is from New York City and taught school for twelve years. She is now writing and editing children's books.  In her free time she enjoys running and riding her bike.

**Reading Consultants**
Kris Flynn, Coordinator, Small School District Literacy, The San Diego County Office of Education

Shelly Forys, Certified Reading Recovery Specialist, W.J. Zahnow Elementary School, Waterloo, IL

Peggy McNamara, Professor, Bank Street College of Education, Reading and Literacy Program